Quantitative Method-Breviary - SPSS

Other publications by Jens K. Perret:

Quantitatives Methoden-Brevier – SPSS   (ISBN: 978-3-748-10761-3)

Arbeitsbuch Makroökonomik und Wirtschaftspolitik   (ISBN: 978-3-662-49624-4)

Knowledge as a driver of Regional Growth in the Russian Federation   (ISBN: 978-3-642-40278-4)

Towards Global Sustainability   (ISBN: 978-3-319-18665-8)

In preparation:

Arbeitsbuch Makroökonomik und Wirtschaftspolitik (2. überarbeitete und ergänzte Auflage)

Arbeitsbuch Statistik für Wirtschafts- und Sozialwissenschaftler

Jens K. Perret

Quantitative Method-Breviary – SPSS

A problem-oriented reference for market researchers

Jens K. Perret
ISM
Im Mediapark 5c
50670 Köln

Bibliografische Information der Deutschen Nationalbibliothek

Die Deutsche Nationalbibliothek verzeichnet diese Publikation in der Deutschen Nationalbibliografie; detaillierte bibliografische Daten sind im Internet über dnb.dnb.de abrufbar.

Original: Quantitatives Methoden-Brevier – SPSS Eine problemorientierte Referenz für Marktforscher

Translation by: Jens K. Perret

© 2018 Jens K. Perret
Printed and published by:
BoD – Books on Demand, Norderstedt
ISBN: 978-3-74813-134-2

Preface

The present breviary sees itself as a compact reference for market or opinion researcher who work with quantitative data. It also lends itself to students of comparable topics. In this last function it can be used to accompany the preparation of a quantitative analysis in the course of a thesis, term paper or practical workshop.

From a methodical standpoint it recapitulates those approaches of quantitative data analysis that are taught in advanced master or MBA study programs at universities or universities of applied sciences. This book in particular is the comprised version of a number of lectures from quantitative market research and applied statistics that the author has taught since 2015 at the International of Management in Cologne.

The breviary is based on the software package SPSS 23 by IBM. It can, however, be used without complications as well with the newer version 24 or 25 or older versions as most of the discussed topics are to be considered established methods of data analysis. As it only offers a compact presentation of the topics usually only a single way to solve a problem is presented. As in many contexts SPSS offers multiple approaches to solve the same problems alternative approaches are in no way considered inferior. Similarly, the breviary does only consider the standard analysis and special cases are – if at all - only discussed in passing. For this a more in-depth book would be needed that discusses all particularities of SPSS. The same argument applies as well for the additional video tutorials that complement the different parts of the breviary.

If not stated differently all commands discussed from chapter 2 onwards can be found in the SPSS menu *Analyze*.

Regarding the interpretation of results and significance levels, it needs to be mentioned that a standard significance level of 5% is assumed. This needs to be changed manually if weak significance (10%) or strong significance (1%) are considered. Similarly, the interpretation is based on two-sided test results as presented by SPSS. For one-sided test results the significance levels would have to be changed (halved) accordingly.

Finally, I wish you dear reader good luck with your research endeavors and that you could make good use of this breviary.

Wuppertal, October 2018   Jens K. Perret

Contents

1 Basics of Data Management

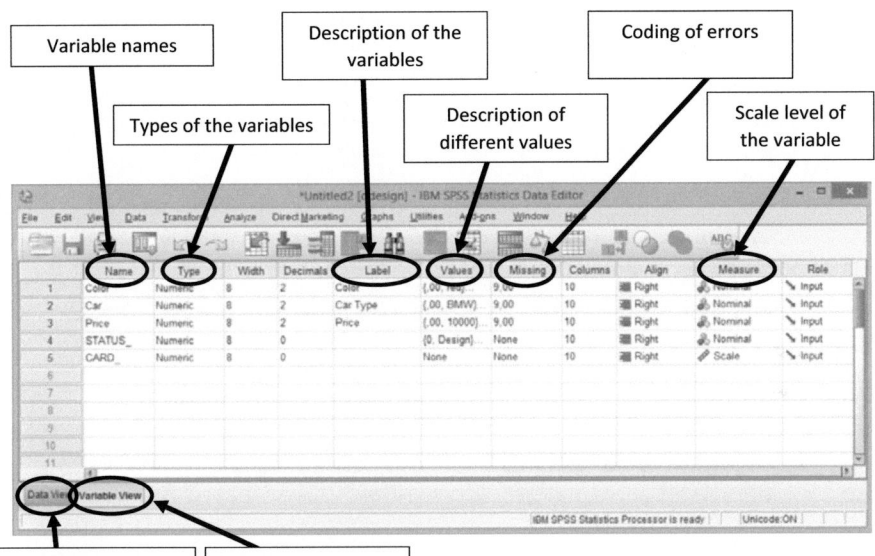

Variable names: As short as possible, no special characters, spaces are not allowed
                       Recommendation: Realize a link to the questions from the questionnaire

Variable types: Numeric – Numbers that can be processed statistically
                       String – Text for which only frequencies can be calculated
                       Recommendation: Test external data sets for a correct conversion of data
                       types (numbers are numeric)

Labels: Detailed description what the variable measures
                       Recommendation: (Short version) Questions from the questionnaire

Value labels: What do the different values represent?
                       Recommendation: All possible values are coded, even those not realized in
                       this sample

Missing values: Which numbers are used to code missing values
                       Recommendation: Code different types of missing values with different
                       numbers (no answer, wrong answer, multiple answers)

Scale levels: Nominal: Only frequencies are possible
                       Ordinal: Characteristics can be ordered
                       Scale/Metric: Distance between characteristics can be interpreted

Data view: Display of the data set like in a spreadsheet editor (Excel)

Variable view: Characteristics of the different variables

Analyze only a select group of cases   **(Data / Select Cases)**
    1) Cases with specific characteristics   (If condition is satisfied)
        -     equal or unequal   = or ~=
        -     logical and resp. or   & or |
    2) Draw a random sample   (Random sample of cases)
    3) After the analysis activate again all cases   (All cases)

Analyze a number of groups at once   **(Data / Split File)**
    1) Each group separately   (Organize output by groups)
    2) All groups in a large table   (Compare groups)

Calculate a new variable   **(Transform / Compute Variable)**

Classify data   **(Transf. / Recode into different Variable)**
    1) Set a new name   (Output variable / Name)
    2) Set a new label   (Output variable / Label)
    3) Generate values   (Old and New Values)

Multiple responses   **(Analyze / Multiple Response)**

    1) Define answer sets   (Ana. / Mult. / Define Variable Set)
        -     What counts as checked?   (Variables are coded as / Counted Value)
        -     Generate set   (Add)
    2) Univariate Frequencies   (Analyze / Multiple Response / Frequencies)
    3) Bivariate Cross Tables   (Analyze / Multiple Response / Crosstabs)

2 Descriptive Statistics

2.1 Univariate Measures

Measures of central tendency and statistical distribution   (Descriptive Statistics)
1) **Measures of Central Tendency**
   - Mode   (Frequencies / Statistics / Central Tendency)
     If the mode is not unique SPSS reports the smallest possible value.
   - Median   (Frequencies / Statistics / Central Tendency)
   - Mean   (Frequencies / Statistics / Central Tendency)
   - Percentiles   (Frequencies / Statistics / Percentiles)
2) **Measures of statistical distribution**
   - Standard deviation   (Frequencies / Statistics / Dispersion)
     SPSS reports the corrected sample standard deviation
   - Variance   (Frequencies / Statistics / Dispersion)
     SPSS reports the corrected sample variance
3) **Measures of dispersion**
   - Skewness   (Frequencies / Statistics / Distribution)
     Result < 0 => leftwards skewed / Result = 0 => symmetrical /
     Result > 0 => rightwards skewed
   - Kurtosis   (Frequencies / Statistics / Distribution)
     Result > 3 => leptokurtic (steep) / Result = 3 => normal distributed /
     Result < 3 => platycurtic (flat)

Statistics

Age

N	Valid	1000
	Missing	0
Mean		38,157
Median		37,000
Mode		24,0[a]
Std. Deviation		14,1047
Variance		198,941
Skewness		,591
Std. Error of Skewness		,077
Kurtosis		-,272
Std. Error of Kurtosis		,155

a. Multiple modes exist. The
smallest value is shown

Measures of central tendency and distribution and boxplots   (Descriptive Statistics / Explore)
1) **Measures of c.t. and dist.**   (Automatically)
2) **Boxplot**   (Automatically)
3) **Stem-Leaf-Diagram**   (Automatically)
4) **Analysis of Outliers**   (Statistics / Outliers)

2.2 Cross Tables and Correspondence Analysis

Cross- / Contingency tables
1) **Generate tables**
2) **Expected frequencies**
3) **Relative values**

(Descriptive Statistics / Crosstabs)
(Automatically)
(Cells / Expected)
(Cells / Percentages / Total)

Sex * Marital status Crosstabulation

| | | | Marital status | | | | Total |
			Single	Married	Divorced	Widowed	
Sex	Male	Count	290	167	4	2	463
		Expected Count	280,1	175,9	3,7	3,2	463,0
		% of Total	29,0%	16,7%	0,4%	0,2%	46,3%
	Female	Count	315	213	4	5	537
		Expected Count	324,9	204,1	4,3	3,8	537,0
		% of Total	31,5%	21,3%	0,4%	0,5%	53,7%
Total		Count	605	380	8	7	1000
		Expected Count	605,0	380,0	8,0	7,0	1000,0
		% of Total	60,5%	38,0%	0,8%	0,7%	100,0%

Absolute / actual values

Expected values

Relative values

Correspondence Analysis
1) **Set rows and columns**
2) **Generate Row or Column Plots**

(Dimension Reduction / Correspondence Analysis)
(At least three characteristics per variable)
(Plots / Row Points, Column Points)

2.3 Measures of Association

What is the weakest scale? – Nominal

    χ2-Test   (Desc. Statistics / Crosstabs / Statistics / Chi2)

    (H_0: The two variables are not related.)

    Contingency Coefficient   (Desc. Stat. / Crosstabs / Statistics / Cont. Coeff.)

    (H_0: The two variables are not related.)

    Cramers V   (Desc. Stat. / Crosstabs / Stat. / Phi and Cramer's V)

    (H_0: The two variables are not related.)

Chi-Square Tests

	Value	df	Asymp. Sig. (2-sided)	
Pearson Chi-Square	2,424[a]	3	,489	→ Significant relation if < 0.05
Likelihood Ratio	2,463	3	,482	
Linear-by-Linear Association	1,944	1	,163	
N of Valid Cases	1000			

a. 4 cells (50,0%) have expected count less than 5. The minimum expected count is 3,24.

Symmetric Measures

		Value	Approximate Significance	
Nominal by Nominal	Phi	,016	,784	Significant relation if < 0.05
	Cramer's V	,016	,784	
	Contingency Coefficient	,016	,784	
N of Valid Cases		284		

What is the weakest scale? – Ordinal

Spearman's Rank-Correlation Coeff.   (Correlate / Bivariate / Spearman)

(H_0: The two variables do not correlate.)

Correlations

			I love to buy cloths.	Age categorized
Spearman's rho	I love to buy cloths.	Correlation Coefficient	1,000	013
		Sig. (2-tailed)	.	,680
		N	1000	1000
	Age categorized	Correlation Coefficient	013	1,000
		Sig. (2-tailed)	,680	.
		N	1000	1000

Significant relation if < 0.05

Correlations

			I love to buy cloths.	Age categorized
Spearman's rho	I love to buy cloths.	Correlation Coefficient	1,000	,013
		Sig. (2-tailed)	.	,680
		N	1000	1000
	Age categorized	Correlation Coefficient	,013	1,000
		Sig. (2-tailed)	,680	.
		N	1000	1000

Strength of the relation

What is the weakest scale? – Metric

Pearson's Correlation Coefficient   (Correlate / Bivariate / Pearson)

(H_0: The two variables do not correlate.)

Correlations

		Age	Income
Age	Pearson Correlation	1	,691**
	Sig. (2-tailed)		,000
	N	1000	1000
Income	Pearson Correlation	,691**	1
	Sig. (2-tailed)	,000	
	N	1000	1000

**. Correlation is significant at the 0.01 level (2-tailed).

Significant correlations report one * (< 0.05) or two ** (< 0.01)

3 Nonparametric Tests and Comparing Means

3.1 Nonparametric Tests – Distribution Tests

Distribution Tests   **(Nonparametric Tests)**

1) **Should the test be for a specific (standard) distribution?**
   - **Test for Binomial distribution**   (Legacy Dialogs / Binomial)

   (H$_0$: The variable is binomially distributed.)

> < 0.05 => not binomially distributed /
> > 0.05 => binomially distributed

Binomial Test

		Category	N	Observed Prop.	Test Prop.	Exact Sig. (2-tailed)
Sex	Group 1	Female	537	,54	,50	,021
	Group 2	Male	463	,46		
	Total		1000	1,00		

- **Test for Normal distribution**   (Legacy Dialogs / 1 Sample K-S)

  (Komogorov-Smirnow-Test / H$_0$: The variable is normally distributed.)

One-Sample Kolmogorov-Smirnov Test

		Age
N		1000
Normal Parameters[a,b]	Mean	38,157
	Std. Deviation	14,1047
Most Extreme Differences	Absolute	,071
	Positive	,071
	Negative	-,058
Test Statistic		,071
Asymp. Sig. (2-tailed)		,000[c]

> < 0.05 => not normally distributed /
> > 0.05 => normally distributed

a. Test distribution is Normal.

b. Calculated from data.

c. Lilliefors Significance Correction.

- **Test for Uniform distribution**   (Legacy Dialogs / 1 Sample K-S)

  (Komogorov-Smirnow-Test / H$_0$: The variable is uniformly distributed.)

One-Sample Kolmogorov-Smirnov Test 2

		Age
N		1000
Uniform Parameters[a,b]	Minimum	16,0
	Maximum	78,0
Most Extreme Differences	Absolute	,263
	Positive	,263
	Negative	-,007
Kolmogorov-Smirnov Z		8,313
Asymp. Sig. (2-tailed)		,000

> < 0.05 => not uniformly distributed /
> > 0.05 => uniformly distributed

a. Test distribution is Uniform.

b. Calculated from data.

- **Test for Exponential distribution** (Legacy dialogs / 1 Sample K-S)
  (Komogorov-Smirnow-Test / H_0: The variable is exponentially distributed.)

One-Sample Kolmogorov-Smirnov Test 3

		Age
N		1000
Exponential parameter. a, b	Mean	38,157
Most Extreme Differences	Absolute	,351
	Positive	,137
	Negative	-,351
Kolmogorov-Smirnov Z		11,102
Asymp. Sig. (2-tailed)		,000

< 0.05 => not exponentially distributed /
> 0.05 => exponentially distributed

a. Test Distribution is Exponential.

b. Calculated from data.

2) **Should the variable be tested for a specifically defined distribution? (Goodness-of-Fit-Test)**
   - Calculate expected values   (Not automatically/ i.e. in Excel)
   - **Goodness-of-fit-Test**   (Legacy Dialogs / Chi-Square)
   (H_0: The variable follows the given distribution.)

Test Statistics

	I love to buy cloths.
Chi-Square	811,824[a]
df	4
Asymp. Sig.	,000

< 0.05 => does not follow the given distribution /
> 0.05 => does follow the given distribution

a. 0 cells (0,0%) have
expected frequencies less
than 5. The minimum
expected cell frequency is
50,0.

3) **Should two variables be tested for a common distribution?**
   - **Homogeneity Test**   (Independent Samples)
   (H_0: The variables share the same distribution.)

Hypothesis Test Summary

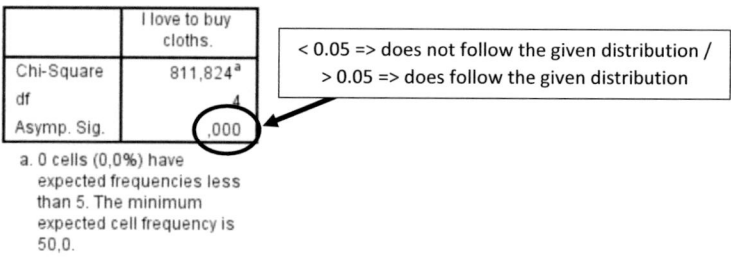

	Null Hypothesis	Test	Sig.	Decision
1	The distribution of Income is the same across categories of Sex.	Independent-Samples Mann-Whitney U Test	,000	Reject the null hypothesis.

Asymptotic significances are displayed. The significance level is ,05.

< 0.05 => Samples have different
distributions /
> 0.05 => Samples share a common
distribution

3.2 Difference Tests

3.2.1 Nominal Scales (Nonparametric)

1) **One sample / one variable is present.**
   - Calculate expected values   (Not automatically / e.g. prepare in Excel)
   - **χ2-Test**   (Legacy Dialogs / Chi-squared)

   (H_0: The variable follows the given distribution.)

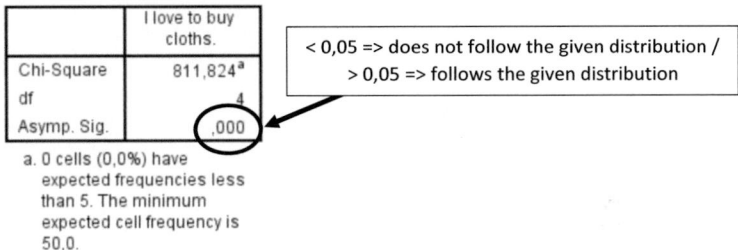

Test Statistics

	I love to buy cloths.
Chi-Square	811,824[a]
df	4
Asymp. Sig.	,000

< 0,05 => does not follow the given distribution /
> 0,05 => follows the given distribution

a. 0 cells (0,0%) have expected frequencies less than 5. The minimum expected cell frequency is 50,0.

2) **One sample with two related / paired data sets.**
   - **McNemar-Test** (dichotomous)   (Legacy Dialogs / Two Related Samples)

   (H_0: The variables share the same distribution.)

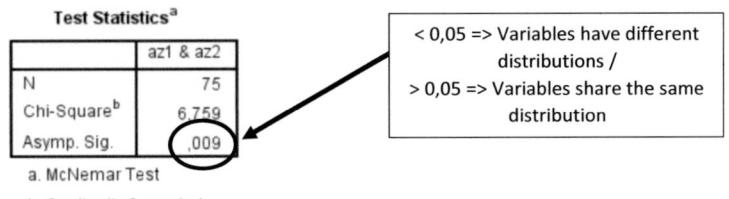

Test Statistics[a]

	az1 & az2
N	75
Chi-Square[b]	6,759
Asymp. Sig.	,009

< 0,05 => Variables have different distributions /
> 0,05 => Variables share the same distribution

a. McNemar Test

b. Continuity Corrected

3) **One sample with more than two related / paired data sets.**
   - **Cochran-Q-Test** (dichotomous)   (Legacy Dialogs / K Related Samples)

   (H_0: The variables share the same distribution.)

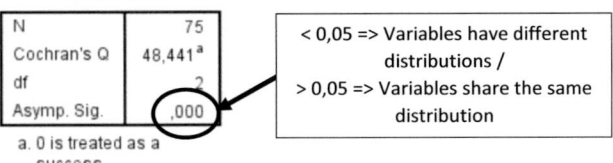

Test Statistics

N	75
Cochran's Q	48,441[a]
df	2
Asymp. Sig.	,000

< 0,05 => Variables have different distributions /
> 0,05 => Variables share the same distribution

a. 0 is treated as a success.

4) Two or more independent samples.

-   **χ2-Test**   (Legacy Dialogs / Chi-squared)

(H$_0$: The variables share the same distribution.)

Test Statistics

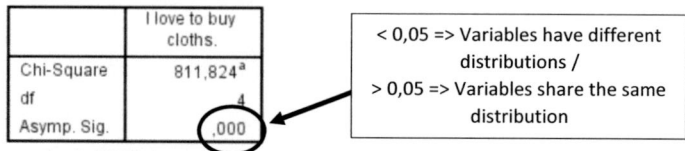

	I love to buy cloths.
Chi-Square	811,824[a]
df	4
Asymp. Sig.	,000

a. 0 cells (0,0%) have expected frequencies less than 5. The minimum expected cell frequency is 50,0.

< 0,05 => Variables have different distributions /
> 0,05 => Variables share the same distribution

3.2.2 Ordinal Scales (Nonparametric)

1) **One sample with two related datasets**
   - **Wilcoxon-Test**   (Legacy Dialogs / Two Related Samples)
   (H_0: The variables share the same distribution.)

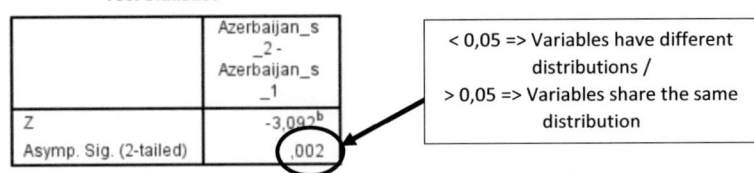

Test Statistics[a]

	Azerbaijan_s_2 - Azerbaijan_s_1
Z	-3,092[b]
Asymp. Sig. (2-tailed)	,002

< 0,05 => Variables have different distributions /
> 0,05 => Variables share the same distribution

a. Wilcoxon Signed Ranks Test

b. Based on positive ranks.

   - **Sign-Test**   (Legacy Dialogs / Two Related Samples)
   (H_0: The variables share the same distribution.)

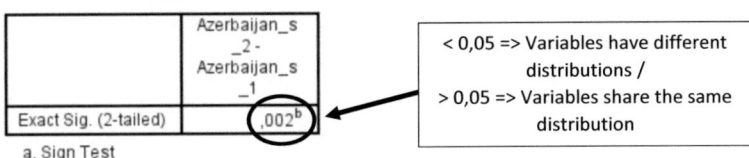

Test Statistics[a]

	Azerbaijan_s_2 - Azerbaijan_s_1
Exact Sig. (2-tailed)	,002[b]

< 0,05 => Variables have different distributions /
> 0,05 => Variables share the same distribution

a. Sign Test

b. Binomial distribution used.

2) **One sample with more than two related datasets**
   - **Kendall-W-Test**   (Legacy Dialogs / K Related Samples)
   (H_0: The variables share the same distribution.)

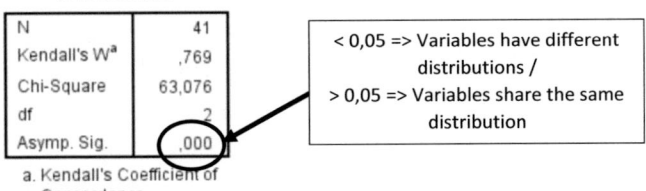

Test Statistics

N	41
Kendall's W[a]	,769
Chi-Square	63,076
df	2
Asymp. Sig.	,000

< 0,05 => Variables have different distributions /
> 0,05 => Variables share the same distribution

a. Kendall's Coefficient of Concordance

3) Two independent samples
- **Whitney-U-Test**   (Legacy Dialogs / 2 Independent Samples)

(H_0: The variables share the same distribution.)

Test Statistics[a]

	Do you follow the ESC events?
Mann-Whitney U	2292,000
Wilcoxon W	12732,000
Z	-,679
Asymp. Sig. (2-tailed)	,497

a. Grouping Variable: Sex

< 0,05 => Variables have different distributions /
> 0,05 => Variables share the same distribution

4) More than two independent samples
- **Kruskal-Wallis-Test**   (Legacy Dialogs / K Independent Samples)

(H_0: The variables share the same distribution.)

Test Statistics[a,b]

	Vorlesungsbesuch
Chi-Square	1,846
df	3
Asymp. Sig.	,605

a. Kruskal Wallis Test

b. Grouping Variable: Konfektionsgröße

< 0,05 => Variables have different distributions /
> 0,05 => Variables share the same distribution

3.2.3 Metric Scales (Comparing Means)

Testing means (t-Test)   **(Compare Means)**
1) **Compare the mean of a variable with a given value**
   - Set test value   (One-Sample t-Test / Test value)
     (H_0: μ = Test value)

One-Sample Test

					95% Confidence Interval of the Difference	
	t	df	Sig. (2-tailed)	Mean Difference	Lower	Upper
Income	6,881	999	,000	73,600	52,61	94,59

< 0.05 => significant deviation from the test value /
> 0.05 => no deviation from the test value

2) **Compare the means of two variables**   (Independent Samples t-Test)
   (H_0: $\mu_1 = \mu_2$)

Independent Samples Test

		Levene's Test for Equality of Variances		t-test for Equality of Means					95% Confidence Interval of the Difference	
		F	Sig.	t	df	Sig. (2-tailed)	Mean Difference	Std. Error Difference	Lower	Upper
Income	Equal variances assumed	,661	,416	5,836	998	,000	123,167	21,106	81,751	164,584
	Equal variances not assumed			5,821	965,704	,000	123,167	21,160	81,643	164,692

< 0.05 => Inequality of variances (2. Row) /
> 0.05 => Equality of variances (1. Row)

< 0.05 => Different means /
> 0.05 => identical means

3) **Compare the means at two points in time / same group**
   (Paired-Samples t-Test)
   (H_0: $\mu_1 = \mu_2$)

Paired Samples Test

		Paired Differences			95% Confidence Interval of the Difference				
		Mean	Std. Deviation	Std. Error Mean	Lower	Upper	t	df	Sig. (2-tailed)
Pair 1	Happiness before eating lunch - Happiness after eating lunch	,45000	1,63755	,36617	-,31640	1,21640	1,229	19	,234

< 0.05 => significant differences between the two points in time /
> 0.05 => no difference between the two points in time

4 Variance Analysis

4.1 Univariate Variance Analysis

1) **Grouping takes place according to what criterion? What is the grouping variable?**
2) **How many factors exist?**
   - 1 then use 1 Factor Variance Analysis
   - > 1 then use Multi-factor Variance Analysis

Univariate Variance Analysis – 1 Factor   (Compare Means / One-Way ANOVA)

1) **Test for differences in the variances of the groups**
   - **Levene Test**   (Options / Homogeneity of variance test)
     $(H_0: \sigma^2_1 = \sigma^2_2)$

   Test of Homogeneity of Variances

   Income

Levene Statistic	df1	df2	Sig
,593	3	996	,620

   < 0.05 => Variance inequality / >
   0.05 => Variance equality

2) **Variance decomposition**
   - **F-Test**   (Automatically)
     $(H_0: \sigma^2_B \leq \sigma^2_W)$

   ANOVA

   Income

	Sum of Squares	df	Mean Square	F	Sig
Between Groups	13657654,43	3	4552551,476	45,053	,000
Within Groups	100645385,6	996	101049,584		
Total	114303040,0	999			

   < 0.05 => significant differences between the groups /
   > 0.05 => no differences between the groups

3) Pairwise comparisons (at least three groups)
- **Scheffé Test**   (Post-Hoc / Scheffé)

$(H_0: \mu_1 = \mu_2)$

< 0.05 => significant differences between the groups /
> 0.05 => no differences between the groups

Dependent Variable: Income

Scheffe

(I) Marital status	(J) Marital status	Mean Difference (I-J)	Std. Error	Sig.	95% Confidence Interval	
					Lower Bound	Upper Bound
Single	Married	-240,422*	20,807	,000	-298,69	-182,16
	Divorced	-168,843	113,129	,527	-485,64	147,95
	Widowed	38,300	120,842	,992	-300,09	376,69
Married	Single	240,422*	20,807	,000	182,16	298,69
	Divorced	71,579	113,565	,941	-246,44	389,59
	Widowed	278,722	121,250	,153	-60,81	618,25
Divorced	Single	168,843	113,129	,527	-147,95	485,64
	Married	-71,579	113,565	,941	-389,59	246,44
	Widowed	207,143	164,520	,663	-253,56	667,84
Widowed	Single	-38,300	120,842	,992	-376,69	300,09
	Married	-278,722	121,250	,153	-618,25	60,81
	Divorced	-207,143	164,520	,663	-667,84	253,56

*. The mean difference is significant at the 0.05 level.

4) Grouping (at least three groups)
- **Scheffé Test**   (Post-Hoc / Scheffé)

Income

Scheffe[a,b]

Marital status	N	Subset for alpha = 0.05
		1
Widowed	7	1442,86
Single	605	1481,16
Divorced	8	1650,00
Married	380	1721,58
Sig.		,131

< 0.05 => Subset is homogeneous /
> 0.05 => Subset is heterogeneous

Means for groups in homogeneous subsets are displayed.

a. Uses Harmonic Mean Sample Size = 14,698.

b. The group sizes are unequal. The harmonic mean of the group sizes is used. Type I error levels are not guaranteed.

4.2 Univariate Variance Analysis Multifactor

Univariate Variance Analysis Multi-factor   **(General Linear Model / Univariate)**
   1) Test for differences in the variances of the groups
       - **Levene Test**   (Options / Homogeneity tests)
        ($H_0: \sigma^2_1 = \sigma^2_2$)

**Levene-Test auf Gleichheit der
Fehlervarianzen[a]**

Abhängige Variable: Einkommen

F	df1	df2	Sig.
1,567	9	990	,120

< 0.05 => Varianceequality /
> 0.05 => Varianceinequality

Testet die Nullhypothese, dass die
Fehlervarianz der abhängigen Variablen über
Gruppen hinweg gleich ist.

a. Design: Konstanter Term + Q01 + Alter_kat
   + Q01 * Alter_kat

   2) Variance decomposition
       - **F-Test**   (Automatically)
        ($H_0: \sigma^2_B \le \sigma^2_W$)
       - **Interaction effects**   (Automatically)
        ($H_0: \sigma^2_B \le \sigma^2_W$)

< 0.05 => direct effects are significant / >
0.05 => direct effects are insignificant

Tests of Between-Subjects Effects

Dependent Variable: Income

Source	Type III Sum of Squares	df	Mean Square	F	Sig.
Corrected Model	55068930,1[a]	7	7866990,019	131,749	,000
Intercept	2389352118	1	2389352118	40014,737	,000
Q01	4550136,068	1	4550136,068	76,202	,000
Age_cat	51179518,56	3	17059839,52	285,703	,000
Q01 * Age_cat	170556,359	3	56852,120	,952	,415
Error	59234109,87	992	59711,804		
Total	2590520000	1000			
Corrected Total	114303040,0	999			

a. R Squared = ,482 (Adjusted R Squared = ,478)

< 0.05 => Interaction effect is significant / >
0.05 => Interaction effect is insignificant

3) Analyze direct and interactione effects
- Draw **effect lines** (Diagrams)
  (all combinations)
- Interpret effect lines ->   Interaction effects can always be interpreted
  Lines do not intersect ->   Direct effect (separate lines) can be interpreted
  Lines do intersect ->   Direct effect (separate lines) cannot be interpreted

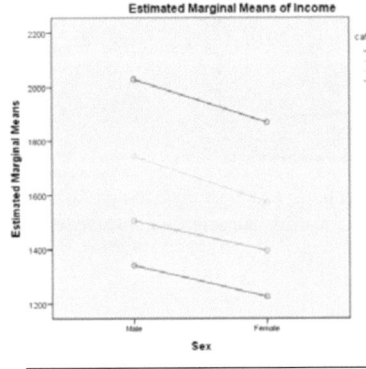

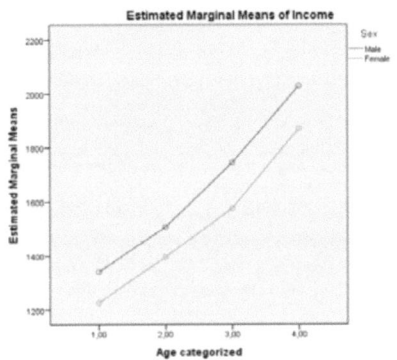

Lines do not intersect =>
Age can be interpreted

Lines do not intersect =>
Sex can be interpreted

4) Pairwise comparisons (at least three groups)
- **Scheffé Test**   (Post-Hoc / Scheffé)
  ($H_0: \mu_1 = \mu_2$)

< 0.05 => significant differences between the groups /
> 0.05 => no differences between the groups

Dependent Variable: Income

Scheffe

(I) Age categorized	(J) Age categorized	Mean Difference (I-J)	Std. Error	Sig.	95% Confidence Interval Lower Bound	Upper Bound
1,00	2,00	-163,50*	22,496	,000	-226,50	-100,51
	3,00	-364,85*	21,422	,000	-424,84	-304,86
	4,00	-658,76*	24,324	,000	-726,88	-590,65
2,00	1,00	163,50*	22,496	,000	100,51	226,50
	3,00	-201,35*	20,172	,000	-257,83	-144,86
	4,00	-495,26*	23,231	,000	-560,31	-430,21
3,00	1,00	364,85*	21,422	,000	304,86	424,84
	2,00	201,35*	20,172	,000	144,86	257,83
	4,00	-293,91*	22,192	,000	-356,06	-231,77
4,00	1,00	658,76*	24,324	,000	590,65	726,88
	2,00	495,26*	23,231	,000	430,21	560,31
	3,00	293,91*	22,192	,000	231,77	356,06

Based on observed means.
The error term is Mean Square(Error) = 59711,804.

*. The mean difference is significant at the ,05 level.

5) Grouping (at least three groups)
- **Scheffé Test**   (Post-Hoc / Scheffé)

Income

Scheffe[a,b,c]

Age categorized	N	Subset			
		1	2	3	4
1,00	214	1283,64			
2,00	263		1447,15		
3,00	332			1648,49	
4,00	191				1942,41
Sig.		1,000	1,000	1,000	1,000

Means for groups in homogeneous subsets are displayed.
Based on observed means.
The error term is Mean Square(Error) = 59711,804.

a. Uses Harmonic Mean Sample Size = 239,194.

b. The group sizes are unequal. The harmonic mean of the group sizes is
   used. Type I error levels are not guaranteed.

c. Alpha = ,05.

< 0.05 => Subsets are heterogeneous /
> 0.05 => Subsets are homogeneous

5 Regression and Prognoses

5.1 Linear Regression

Linear Regression   **(Regression / Linear)**
1) **Significance of the coefficients**
   - **t-Test**   (Automatically)
     (H_0: $b_i = 0$)

| < 0.05 => coefficient is different from 0 / |
| > 0.05 => coefficient can be 0 |

Coefficients[a]

Model		Unstandardized Coefficients		Standardized Coefficients	t	Sig.	Collinearity Statistics	
		B	Std. Error	Beta			Tolerance	VIF
1	(Constant)	1009,280	22,780		44,306	,000		
	Age	16,675	,528	,695	31,558	,000	,999	1,001
	Sex	-134,012	14,940	-,198	-8,970	,000	,999	1,001

a. Dependent Variable: Income

| (Absolute) size determines the importance the variable | | < 10 /(2) => No problem with multicollinearity / > 10 (2) => Significant multicollinearity present |

2) **Quality of the overall regression (model)**
   - **R² or corrected R²**   (Automatically)
     (as large as possible, as close to 1 as possible)

| = 2 => no problem with autocorrelation / significantly > 2 or < 2 => autocorrelation exists |

Model Summary[b]

Model	R	R Square	Adjusted R Square	Std. Error of the Estimate	Durbin-Watson
1	,718[a]	,516	,515	235,505	2,037

a. Predictors: (Constant), Sex, Age

b. Dependent Variable: Income

| Share of the dependent variable's variance that is explained via the regression line / As large and as close to 1 as possible | | Corrected for the number of used variables |

   - **F-Test**   (Automatically)
     (H_0: $b_1 = ... = b_n = 0$ / H_0: $\sigma^2_{Regression} \geq \sigma^2_{Residuals}$)

ANOVA[a]

Model		Sum of Squares	df	Mean Square	F	Sig.
1	Regression	59006785,80	2	29503392,90	531,951	,000[b]
	Residual	55296254,20	997	55462,642		
	Total	114303040,0	999			

a. Dependent Variable: Income

b. Predictors: (Constant), Sex, Age

| Can be used to compare two elsewise identical models. Larger = better | | < 0.05 => Model has significant explanatory power / > 0.05 => Model has no explanatory power |

3) **Additional quality indicators**
   - **Autocorrelation -> Durbin Watson** (Statistics / Durbin-Watson)
     (as close to 2 as possible)
   - **Multicollinearity -> VIF**   (Statistics / Collinearity diagnostics)
     (Smaller than 10 (2 is possible), as close to 1 as possible)
4) **Order of importance of the variables**
   - **Beta-Coefficients**   (Automatically)
     (The larger the more important the variable is in the model)
5) **Adjust the model**
6) **Formulate the model and interpret it**

Non-linear Regression   (Regression / Curve Estimation)
Choice of model type   (Models)

Model Summary and Parameter Estimates

Dependent Variable: Gewicht in kg

Equation	Model Summary					Parameter Estimates			
	R Square	F	df1	df2	Sig.	Constant	b1	b2	b3
Linear	,482	262,458	1	282	,000	-97,866	,943		
Quadratic	,483	131,456	2	281	,000	-241,778	2,583	-,005	
Cubic	,484	131,528	2	281	,000	-199,113	1,808	,000	-9,295E-6
S	,516	300,429	1	282	,000	6,684	-434,993		

The independent variable is Größe in cm.

As large and as close to 1 as possible

< 0.05 => Model has significant explanatory power /
> 0.05 => Model has not explanatory power

As large as possible

5.2 Time Series

Analysis of Time Series and Forecasts

1) Select seasonality   (Data / Define Date and Time)
   - Select fitting format of data
   - Select starting period
2) Set seasonality   (Analyze / Forecasting / Seasonal Decomposition)
   - Set time series variables
   - Select type of model
3) Set type of model   (Analyze / Forecasting / Create Traditional Models)
   Select method:
      Exponential Smoothing
      - Select type   (Variables / Criteria / Model Type)
      ARIMA
      - Select type   (Variables / Criteria / ARIMA-Orders)
4) Set other options
   - **Display Autocorrelationfunction**   (Analyze / Forecasting / Autocorrelations)
   - Display original values   (Automatically)
   - Display estimates   (Plots / Fit Values)
   - Display forecasts   (Automatically)
   - Confidence intervals forecasts   (Plots / Conf. Intervals for Forecasts)
5) Set interval of forecasts
   - Set final period   (Options / Forecast period)
6) Save the model
   Set file name   (Save / Export Model File)

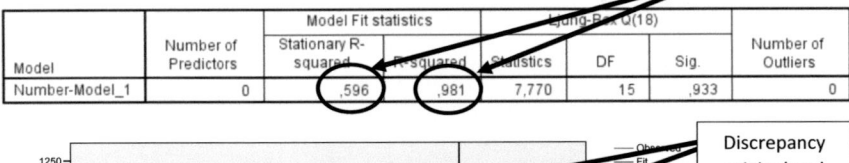

Model Statistics

As large as possible, as close to 1 as possible

Model	Number of Predictors	Model Fit statistics		Ljung-Box Q(18)			Number of Outliers
		Stationary R-squared	R-squared	Statistics	DF	Sig.	
Number-Model_1	0	,596	,981	7,770	15	,933	0

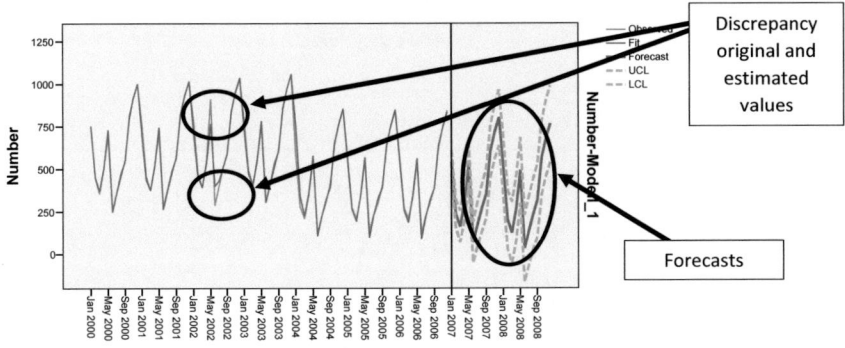

Discrepancy original and estimated values

Forecasts

6 Discriminant Analysis

Discriminant Analysis   **(Classify / Discriminant)**
1) **Whereby should the grouping take place? What is the grouping variable?**
2) **Quality of the analysis**
   - **Eigenvalue**   (Automatically)
     (As large as possible, as close to 1 as possible)
   - **Wilk's Lambda**   (Automatically)
     (As small as possible, as close to 0 as possible / H_0: Wilks $\lambda = 0$)
   - **Can. Correlation Coefficient**   (Automatically)
     (As large as possible, as close to 1 as possible)

> As large as possible, as close to 1 as possible

Eigenvalues

Function	Eigenvalue	% of Variance	Cumulative %	Canonical Correlation
1	,081 [a]	100,0	100,0	,274

a. First 1 canonical discriminant functions were used in the analysis.

> As large as possible, as close to 1 as possible

Wilks' Lambda

> As small as possible, as close to 0 as possible

Test of Function(s)	Wilks' Lambda	Chi-square	df	Sig.
1	,925	77,911	2	,000

> < 0.05 => Dataset is not suited for the analysis/
> > 0.05 => Dataset is suited for discriminant analysis

3) **Estimate discriminant function**
4) **Illustrate the importance the different variables**
   - **Standardize coefficients**   (Automatically)
     (Je größer umso höher die Bedeutung)
5) Estimate classification functions
6) **Classify cases**   (Classify / Summary Table)
   - Fehlereinordnung und Bewerten

> Probability that the assigned group is the correct one

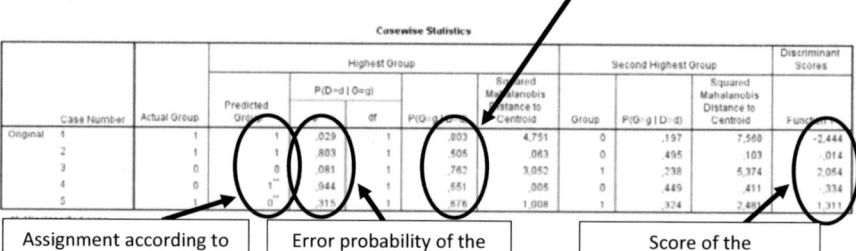

Casewise Statistics

| Case Number | Actual Group | Highest Group | | | | | Second Highest Group | | | Discriminant Scores |
		Predicted Group	P(D>d | G=g)	df	P(G=g | D=d)	Squared Mahalanobis Distance to Centroid	Group	P(G=g | D=d)	Squared Mahalanobis Distance to Centroid	Function 1
Original 1	1	1	,029	1	,803	4,751	0	,197	7,568	-2,444
2	1	1	,803	1	,505	,063	0	,495	,103	,014
3	0	0	,081	1	,762	3,052	1	,238	5,374	2,054
4	0	1	,944	1	,551	,005	0	,449	,411	,334
5	1	0	,315	1	,876	1,008	1	,324	2,485	1,311

> Assignment according to classification function

> Error probability of the assignment

> Score of the diskriminant function

Classification Results[a]

		Sex	Predicted Group Membership		Total
			Male	Female	
Original	Count	Male	289	174	463
		Female	216	321	537
	%	Male	62,4	37,6	100,0
		Female	40,2	59,8	100,0

a. 61,0% of original grouped cases correctly classified.

Quality of the assignment
Reference is 1/number of groups

7 Exploratory Factor Analysis

Factor Analysis   **(Dimension Reduction / Factor)**

1) **Quality of the Factor Analysis**
   - **Communalities**   (Automatically)
     (At least 0.5)

Communalities

	Initial	Extraction
When I hear that a new type of clothing (new style) is available I am directly interested in buying it.	1,000	,601
I love to buy cloths.	1,000	,622
I like to buy products by new designers / brands.	1,000	,526
I know about new designers and brands much earlier than others.	1,000	,601

Extraction Method: Principal Component Analysis.

Share of the variance of the variables that is explained by the selected factors / > 0.5

   - **KMO- / Bartlett Test**   (Descriptive Statistics / KMO and Bartlett Test)
     (At least 0.5 / H_0: Communality$_1$ = Communality$_2$ = ... = Communality$_n$ = 0)

KMO and Bartlett's Test

Kaiser-Meyer-Olkin Measure of Sampling Adequacy.		,720
Bartlett's Test of Sphericity	Approx. Chi-Square	1051,235
	df	6
	Sig.	,000

> 0.5 Dataset is usable / < 0.5 Dataset is not

< 0.05 => Dataset is usable / > 0.05 => Dataset is not usable

2) **Number of factors**
   - **Kaiser Criterion**   (Automatically)
     (Number of factors = Number of eigenvalues larger than 1)

Total Variance Explained

Component	Initial Eigenvalues			Extraction Sums of Squared Loadings		
	Total	% of Variance	Cumulative %	Total	% of Variance	Cumulative %
1	2,350	58,752	58,752	2,350	58,752	58,752
2	,768	19,203	77,955			
3	,479	11,965	89,920			
4	,403	10,080	100,000			

Extraction Method: Principal Component Analysis.

Number of eigenvalues > 1 is 1 => Extract 1 factor

Share of total variance explained by the extracted factors, should be > 50%

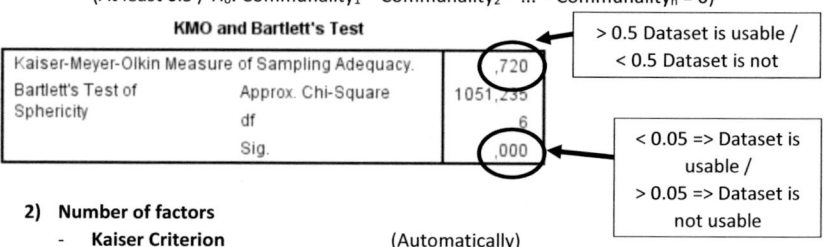

- **Elbow Criterion**   (Extraction / Screeplot)
  (Find the ‚bend' in the screeplot, the number of factors to be extracted is the number to the left of the bend)

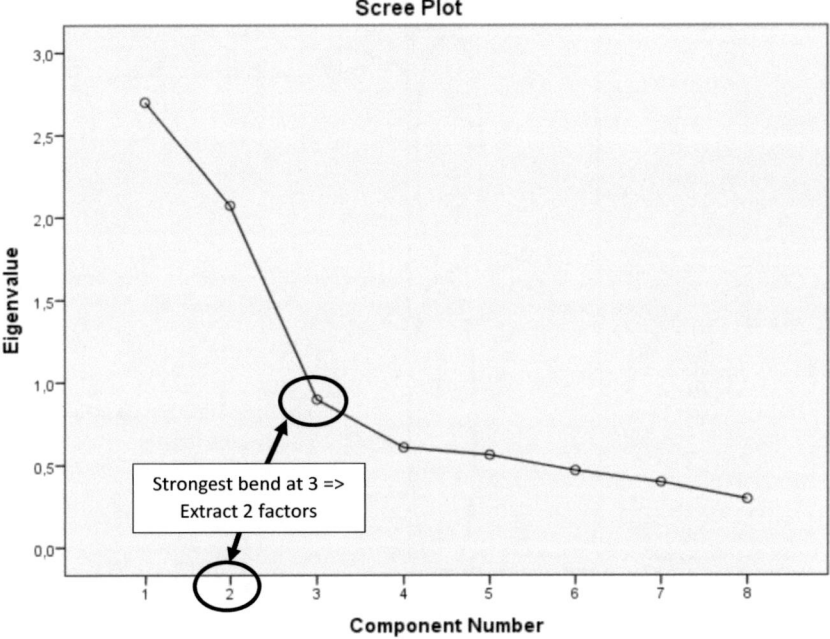

Scree Plot

Strongest bend at 3 =>
Extract 2 factors

3) **Suppress small factor loadings**   (Options / Suppress small coefficients)
4) **Estimate factor loadings**

Component Matrix[a]

	Component
	1
When I hear that a new type of clothing (new style) is available I am directly interested in buying it.	,775
I love to buy cloths.	,789
I like to buy products by new designers / brands.	,725
I know about new designers and brands much earlier than others.	,775

Extraction Method: Principal Component Analysis.

a. 1 components extracted.

5) Rotation of the factor loadings   (Rotation / Varimax)

Rotated Component Matrix^a

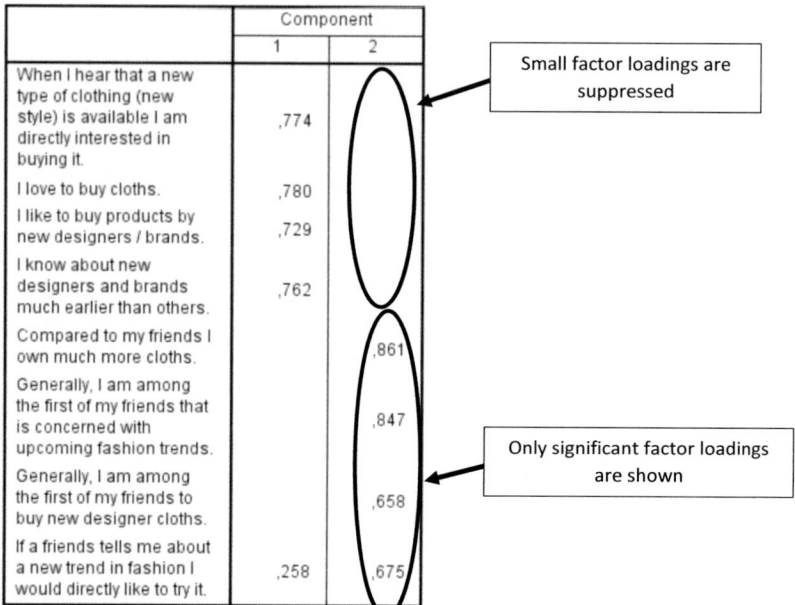

	Component	
	1	2
When I hear that a new type of clothing (new style) is available I am directly interested in buying it.	,774	
I love to buy cloths.	,780	
I like to buy products by new designers / brands.	,729	
I know about new designers and brands much earlier than others.	,762	
Compared to my friends I own much more cloths.		,861
Generally, I am among the first of my friends that is concerned with upcoming fashion trends.		,847
Generally, I am among the first of my friends to buy new designer cloths.		,658
If a friends tells me about a new trend in fashion I would directly like to try it.	,258	,675

Small factor loadings are suppressed

Only significant factor loadings are shown

Extraction Method: Principal Component Analysis.
Rotation Method: Varimax with Kaiser Normalization.

a. Rotation converged in 3 iterations.

6) Save factors   (Save)

7) Interpret factors

8) Illustrate factors graphically   (Rotation / Loading Plots)

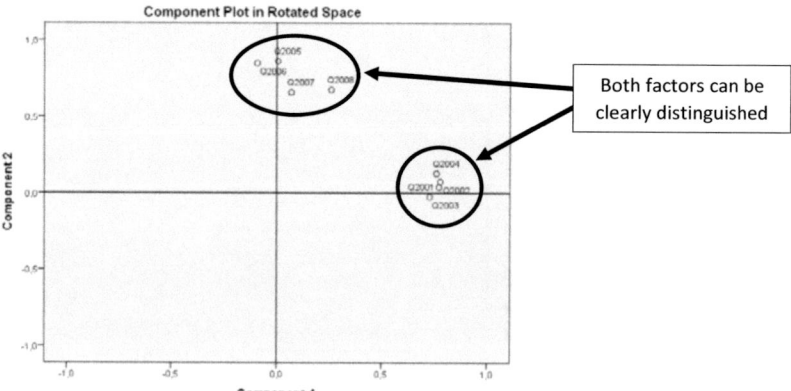

Component Plot in Rotated Space

Both factors can be clearly distinguished

8 Multidimensional Scaling

Multidimensional Scaling   **(Scale / Multidimensional Scaling (PROXSCAL))**
   1) **Standardize variables**   (Measure / Standardize)
   2) **Calculate distances / similarities**   (Measure / Interval)
   - Binary:
      o   Jaccard Coefficient
      o   Simple Matching Coefficient
   - Metric:
      o   City-Block Metric
          (Distances in a grid context)
      o   Euclidean Distance
          (Normal understanding of distance)
      o   Squared Euklidean Distance
          (SPSS Standard)
      o   Minkowski Metric
      o   Q-Correlation Coefficient
          (Measure of similarity)

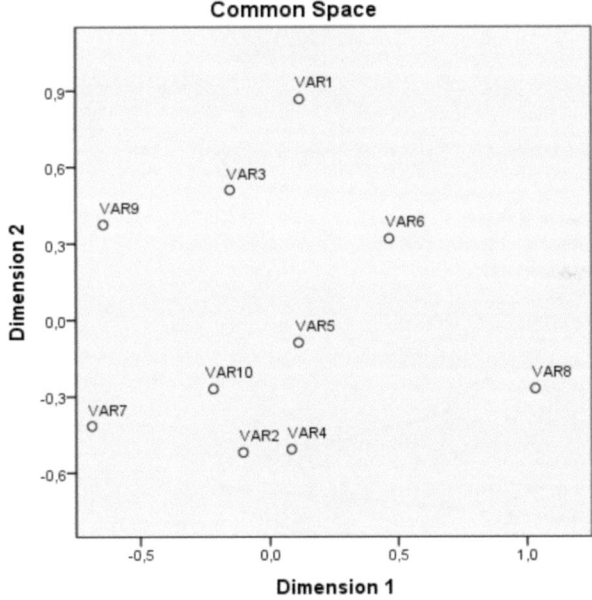

Object Points

Common Space

9 Cluster Analysis

1) **Standardize variables**   (Method / Standardize)
2) **Calculate distances / similarities**   (Method / Interval)
   - Binary (details dee MDS)
   - Metric (details see MDS)
3) **Hierarchical or partitioning**
Hierarchical   **(Classify / Hierarchical Cluster)**
1) **What should be clustered?**   (Cases or variables)
2) **Type of fusion algorithm**   (Method / Cluster Method)
   - **Single Linkage** (Well suited to detect outliers)
     (Shortest distance towards a neighbor / cluster)

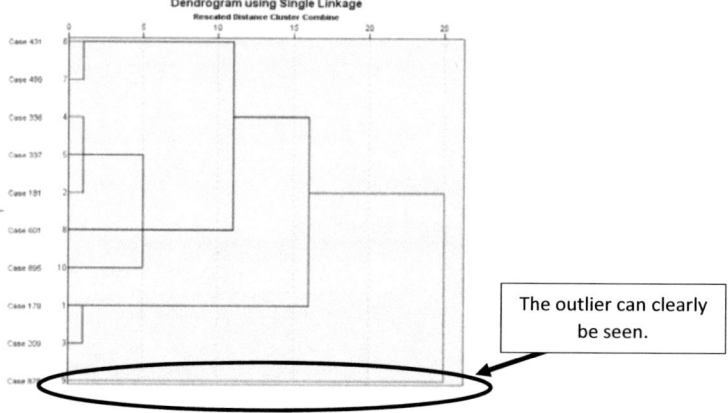

The outlier can clearly be seen.

   - **Complete Linkage**
     (Largest possible distance towards a neighbor / cluster)
   - **Average Linkage**
     (Average distance of all members of a cluster to all members of another cluster)
   - **Ward Methode** (Well suited to find similar sized groups)

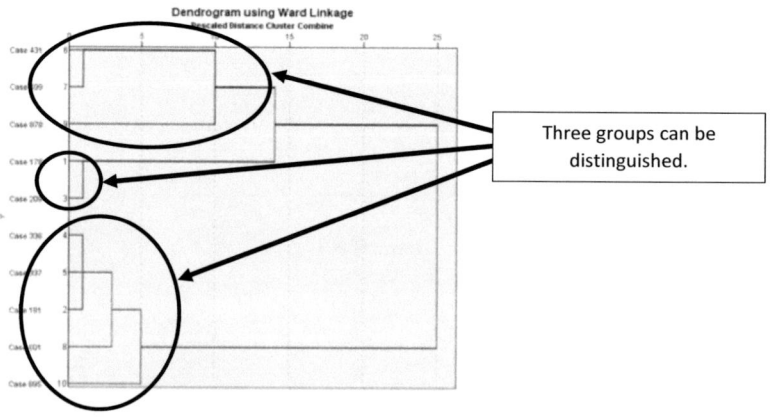

Three groups can be distinguished.

3) Determine ideal number of clusters
- **Dendrogram** (Diagrams / Dendrogram)
- **Levels of aggregation / clustering**
- **Coefficients** (Automatically)

Agglomeration Schedule

Stage	Cluster Combined		Coefficients	Stage Cluster First Appears		Next Stage
	Cluster 1	Cluster 2		Cluster 1	Cluster 2	
1	4	7	,273	0	0	5
2	5	10	,796	0	0	6
3	2	3	2,259	0	0	6
4	1	8	3,740	0	0	8
5	4	6	6,439	1	0	7
6	2	5	9,886	3	2	8
7	4	9	13,603	5	0	9
8	1	2	20,335	4	6	9
9	1	4	36,000	8	7	0

The strongest relative increase takes place from 3 to 2 clusters => Choose the 3 cluster solution

4) Determine cluster memberships (Statistics / Single Solution / Number of Clusters)

Cluster Membership

Case	2 Clusters
1:Case 136	1
2:Case 302	1
3:Case 344	1
4:Case 408	2
5:Case 423	1
6:Case 727	2
7:Case 791	2
8:Case 795	1
9:Case 799	2
10:Case 937	1

Partitioning   **(Classify / K-Means Cluster)**
1) **Determine number of clusters**
2) **Import cluster centers or determine them dynamically**

Final Cluster Centers

	Cluster	
	1	2
When I hear that a new type of clothing (new style) is available I am directly interested in buying it.	5	3
I love to buy cloths.	5	2
I like to buy products by new designers / brands.	5	3
I know about new designers and brands much earlier than others.	4	3

3) **Determine cluster memberships**   (Options / Cluster information for each case)

Cluster Membership

Case Number	Cluster	Distance
136	2	2,528
302	2	1,929
344	2	1,312
408	1	,901
423	2	1,929
727	1	1,953
791	1	1,521
795	2	1,841
799	1	2,194
937	2	2,173

10 Conjoint Analysis

Generate an orthogonal design   (Data / Orthogonal Design / Generate)
1) Add factors
2) Define value labels
3) Set number of cases and test cases   (Options)
4) Save designs   (Data file / Create a new data set)

Display the design   (Data / Orthogonal Design / Display)

Card List

	Card ID	Color	Car Type	Price
1	1	silver	Audi	20000
2	2	red	BMW	15000
3	3	silver	BMW	10000
4	4	red	Toyota	20000
5	5	black	VW	20000
6	6	black	Ford	25000
7	7	black	VW	15000
8	8	black	Audi	10000
9	9	silver	Ford	10000
10	10	red	VW	10000
11	11	black	BMW	20000
12	12	red	Audi	25000
13	13	black	Ford	10000
14	14	black	Toyota	10000
15	15	red	Ford	15000
16	16	black	BMW	25000
17	17	red	Toyota	25000
18	18	red	Audi	10000
19	19	silver	Toyota	15000
20	20	black	Toyota	10000
21	21	silver	VW	25000
22	22	black	Audi	15000
23	23	red	BMW	10000
24	24	red	Ford	20000
25	25	red	VW	10000

For these cases data needs to be collected

Apply Conjoint Analyse
1) Open Syntaxeditor
2) **CONJOINT PLAN='Path+Name of the Design File.sav'**
   /DATA='Path+Name of the data file.sav' /Datatype=Variable1 TO VariableN
   - **Datatype:** SCORE   Variables 1 to n are absolute scores
                  RANK   Variables 1 to n are ranks
                  SEQUENCE   Variables 1 to n contain a sequence ordering the cases

3) Utility values   (Automatically)

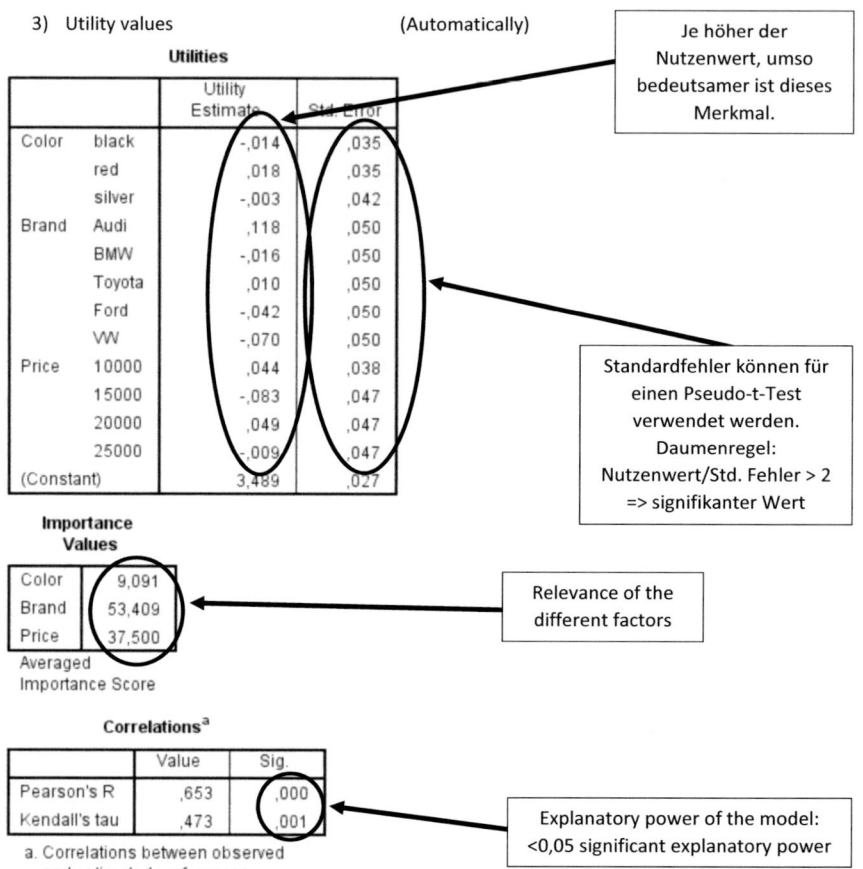

Je höher der Nutzenwert, umso bedeutsamer ist dieses Merkmal.

Utilities

		Utility Estimate	Std. Error
Color	black	-,014	,035
	red	,018	,035
	silver	-,003	,042
Brand	Audi	,118	,050
	BMW	-,016	,050
	Toyota	,010	,050
	Ford	-,042	,050
	VW	-,070	,050
Price	10000	,044	,038
	15000	-,083	,047
	20000	,049	,047
	25000	-,009	,047
(Constant)		3,489	,027

Standardfehler können für einen Pseudo-t-Test verwendet werden. Daumenregel: Nutzenwert/Std. Fehler > 2 => signifikanter Wert

Importance Values

Color	9,091
Brand	53,409
Price	37,500

Averaged Importance Score

Relevance of the different factors

Correlations[a]

	Value	Sig.
Pearson's R	,653	,000
Kendall's tau	,473	,001

a. Correlations between observed and estimated preferences

Explanatory power of the model: <0,05 significant explanatory power

11 Artificial Neural Networks

Artificial Neural Networks   **(Neural Networks / Multilayer Perceptron)**
1) Select independent variables   (Covariates)
2) Set size of the learning and testing set   (Partitions / Partition Dataset)
3) Structure of the Perceptron   (Architecture)
4) Report weights of the network   (Output / Network Structure / Synaptic Weights)
5) Estimate relevance of the factors   (Output / Independent variable importance analysis)

Neural Network and Synaptic Weights:

Parameter Estimates

		Predicted							
		Hidden Layer 1			Output Layer				
Predictor		H(1:1)	H(1:2)	H(1:3)	[f4=2]	[f4=3]	[f4=4]	[f4=5]	[f4=6]
Input Layer	(Bias)	-1,885	-2,028	-1,351					
	f2	,413	-1,276	-3,522					
	f3	4,365	-3,439	,323					
	f5	-,130	-,046	,196					
	f8	,082	,135	-,150					
Hidden Layer 1	(Bias)				-,122	3,882	,562	-,515	-2,382
	H(1:1)				-2,576	-1,044	-2,018	3,198	2,770
	H(1:2)				3,409	,572	-2,798	-1,437	-,359
	H(1:3)				2,816	,989	-1,164	-1,411	-1,607

Classification

		Predicted					Percent
Sample	Observed	S	M	L	XL	XXL	Correct
Training	S	45	4	0	0	0	91,8%
	M	11	30	5	2	0	62,5%
	L	0	5	36	3	0	81,8%
	XL	0	0	0	51	0	100,0%
	XXL	0	0	0	3	0	0,0%
	Overall Percent	28,7%	20,0%	21,0%	30,3%	0,0%	83,1%
Testing	S	18	1	1	0	0	90,0%
	M	3	18	0	0	0	85,7%
	L	0	1	10	2	0	76,9%
	XL	0	0	2	32	0	94,1%
	XXL	0	0	0	1	0	0,0%
	Overall Percent	23,6%	22,5%	14,6%	39,3%	0,0%	87,6%

Dependent Variable: Clothing Size

As high as possible and
possibly similarly sized

Independent Variable Importance

	Importance	Normalized Importance
Height in cm	,445	88,5%
Weight in kg	,503	100,0%
Smoker	,020	4,0%
Happiness	,032	6,4%

Explanatory power of the
independent variables
Higher => more relevant

12 Decision Sheets

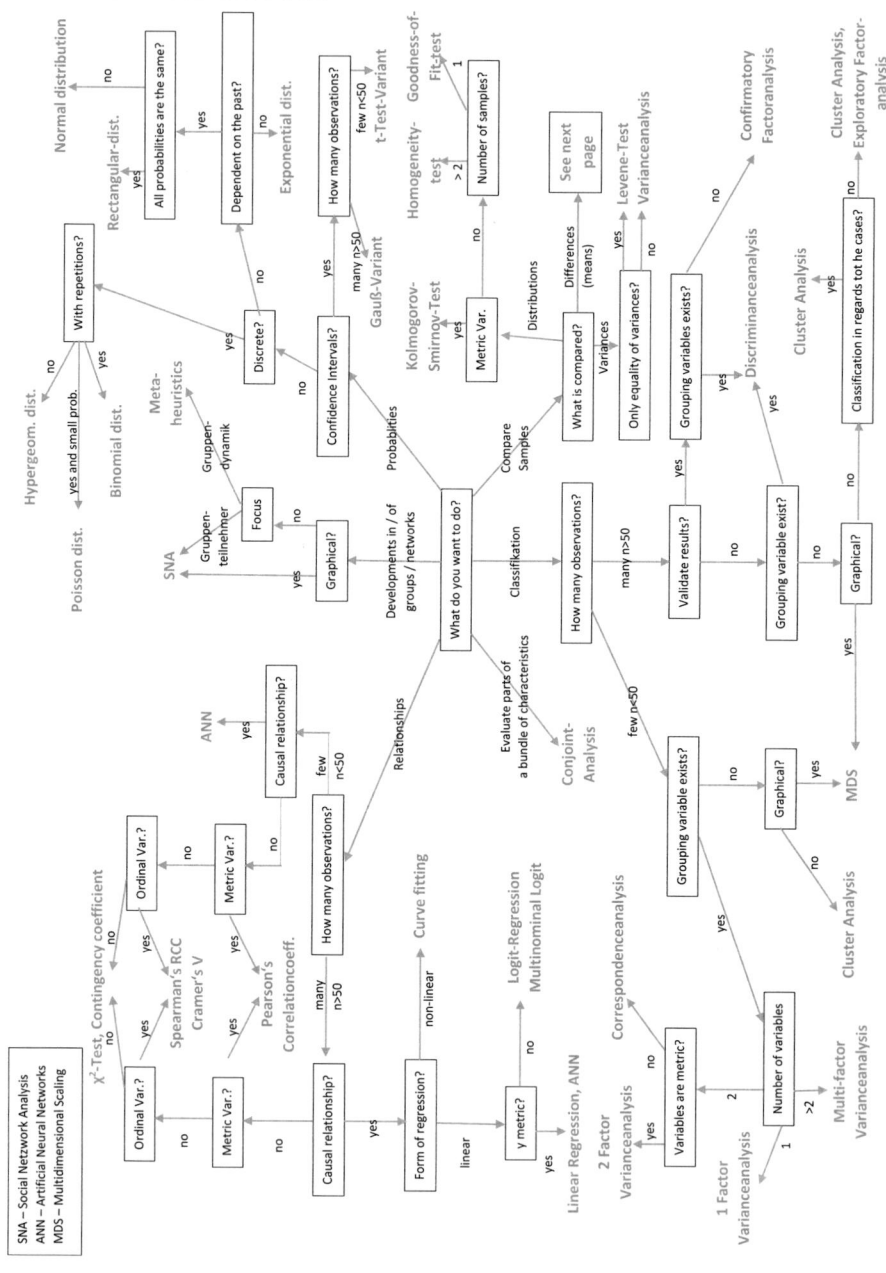

Comparisons / Differences (Means)

Scale level	Samples	Type	Test
Nominal	1	Independent / 1 Variable	Binomial- / χ^2- Test
		Dependent / 2 Variables	NcNemar-Test
		Dependent / > 2 Variables	Cochran-Q-Test
	2		Homogeneity- / χ^2- Test
	> 2		χ^2- Test
Ordinal	1	Dependent / 2 Variables	Wilcoxon- / Sign-Test
		Dependent / >2 Variables	Kendall-W-Test
	2	Independent	Whitney-U-Test
	> 2	Independent	Kruskal-Wallis-H-Test
Metric	1	Varianz bekannt	Gauß-Test
		Varianz unbekannt	1 SP t-Test
		Dependent	2 SP (Dependent) t-Test
	2	Independent	2 SP (Independent) t-Test
	> 2	Independent / 1 Factor	1 Factor ANOVA
		Independent / 2 Factors	2 Factor ANOVA
		Dependent	ANOVA with Repeated

Measures

Scale Level	Measures of Central Tendency	Measures of Dispersion	Measures of Distribution	Measures of Association
Nominal	Mode (most frequent value)	-	-	χ^2-Statistic (Obs. – Exp. Frequencies), Contingency Coeff., Cramer's V (Obs. – Exp. Frequencies)
Ordinal	Median (middle value) / Quartiles / Percentiles / Quantiles (p% are smaller)	Range (Max-Min), Interquartile Range (middle 50%)		Spearman's Rank Correlation Coefficient (Corr. Coefficient for Ranked Data)
Quasi-metric	like metric	like metric	like metric	like metric
Metric	Mean (Average)	Variance (Mean quadratic distance from mean), Standard Deviation (Square root of Variance)	Skewness (More small / large values), Kurtosis (Heterogeneity of observations)	Covariance (Shared Variance), Correlation Coefficient by Pearson (Normalized Covariance)

Univariate Statistics — Bivariate Statistics

Descriptive Statistics

Hypotheses:

H_0-Hypothesis (Nullhypothesis): What is tested.
H_1-Hypothesis (Alternative hypothesis): What we are interested in.

Equality	$(= / \leq / \geq)$	No relation / Association
Inequality	$(\neq / > / <)$	Relation / Association

Significance:

α-Error = Type 1-Error = p-value = significance (level) = Probability that H_0-hypothesis is correct = Error when we assume H_1 to be the correct hypothesis

Significance levels: ≤ 0.1 weakly significant ≤ 0.05 significant ≤ 0.01 highly significant ≤ 0.001 with almost certainty

Two-tailed-tests ($\neq$ versus =) and one-tailed tests (< or > versus $\leq$ or $\geq$)

To switch from the significance for a two-tailed test (SPSS standard) to the significance for a one-tailed test, divide significance by 2.

13 Videotutorials

1 SPSS Basics	Open Datasets
	SPSS Program Surface
	Select Cases
	Generate new Variables
	Multiple Responses
2 Descriptive Statistics	
2.1 Univariate Measures	Univariate Measures
	Exploratory Data Analysis
2.2 Cross-tables and Correspondence Analysis	Cross Tables
	Correspondence Analysis
2.3 Measures of Association	Nominal Scale
	Ordinal Scale
	Metric Scale
3 Non-parametric tests and Comparing Means	
3.1 Non-parametric tests / Distribution tests	Binomial Distribution
	Normal Distribution
	Uniform Distribution
	Exponential Distribution
	Goodness-of-Fit Test
	Homogeneity Test
	χ^2-Test (1 sample / 1 var.)
	McNemar-Test (1 sample / 2 dep. groups)
	Cochran-Q-Test (1 sample / $\geq$ 2 dep. groups)
	χ^2-Test ($\geq$ 2 indep. groups)
	Wilcoxon-Test (2 dep. var.)
	Kendall-W-Test ($\geq$ 2 dep. var.)
	Mann-Whitney-U-Test (2 indep. var.)
	Kruskal-Wallis-Test ($\geq$ 2 indep. var.)
3.2 Comparing Means	Comparing Means (Given value)
	Comparing Means (2 indep. groups)
	Comparing Means (2 dep. groups)
4 Variance Analysis	
4.1 Univariate Variance Analysis – One factor	Variance Analysis (1 factor)
4.2 Univariate Variance Analysis – Multi factor	Variance Analysis ($\geq$ 2 factors)
5 Regression and Prognoses	
5.1 (Linear) Regression	Linear Regression
	Nonlinear Regression
	Logit Regression
5.2 Time Series	Time Series and Prognoses
6 Discriminant Analysis	Discriminant Analysis
7 Exploratory Factor Analysis	Factor Analysis
8 Multidimensional Scaling	Multidimensional Scaling
9 Cluster Analysis	Hierarchical Cluster Analysis
	Partitioning Cluster Analysis
10 Conjoint Analysis	Generating orthogonal design
	Conjoint Analysis
11 Artificial Neural Networks	Artificial Neural Networks

All videos can be accessed via the following Youtube-Channel:

https://statistics.jens-perret.de

Alternatively the following QR-code can be used for access: